better together*

* This book is best read together, grownup and kid.

 akidsco.com

a
kids
book
about

a kids book about

by Elly Both

A Kids Co.
Editor Emma Wolf
Designer Jelani Memory
Creative Director Rick DeLucco
Studio Manager Kenya Feldes
Sales Director Melanie Wilkins
Head of Books Jennifer Goldstein
CEO and Founder Jelani Memory

DK
Editor Emma Roberts
Senior Production Editor Jennifer Murray
Senior Production Controller Louise Minihane
Senior Acquisitions Editor Katy Flint
Acquisitions Project Editor Sara Forster
Managing Art Editor Vicky Short
Managing Director, Licensing Mark Searle
DK would like to thank Dr Cassie Coleman

This American Edition, 2025
Published in the United States by DK Publishing
1745 Broadway, 20th Floor, New York, NY 10019

DK, a Division of Penguin Random House LLC
Text and design copyright © 2023 by A Kids Book About, Inc.
A Kids Book About, Kids Are Ready, and the colophon 'a' are trademarks of A Kids Book About, Inc.
25 26 27 10 9 8 7 6 5 4 3 2 1
001-345778-Feb/2025

A catalog record for this book is available from the Library of Congress.
ISBN: 978-0-5939-6437-8

DK books are available at special discounts when purchased in bulk for
sales promotions, premiums, fund-raising, or educational use. For details, contact:
DK Publishing Special Markets, 1745 Broadway, 20th Floor, New York, NY 10019, or SpecialSales@dk.com

Printed and bound in China

www.dk.com

akidsco.com

MIX
Paper | Supporting
responsible forestry
FSC™ C018179

This book was made with Forest
Stewardship Council™ certified
paper – one small step in DK's
commitment to a sustainable future.
Learn more at www.dk.com/uk/
information/sustainability

This book is dedicated to anyone who finds it hard to focus, sit still, or often finds themselves daydreaming. You are unique and wonderful exactly as you are.

And to Ben, Henry, and Teddy, who inspire me to be my best self.

Intro
for grownups

Think about the kid you're reading with—do they often drift into daydreams or find it hard to focus? Do they find it difficult to sit still, even though they really try? Do they feel like some things are hard for them but easy for other people? It can be really tricky to feel this way, and not understand why.

I sometimes experience these things, too. I used to feel worried and confused until I found out why: I have something called ADHD.

While there are challenges that come along with ADHD, and it's not always easy, my diagnosis has helped me discover the ways I can be my best self. I found my superpower!

Now, I understand myself better and accept myself for who I am.

This book is designed to reach kids who are having a similar experience and help them feel seen and understood. I hope it helps them to celebrate what makes them unique, and discover their own superpower!

Have you heard of **ADHD**?

It has such a **looooooong** name that people often use the first letter of each of its words to make it shorter.

ADHD stands for

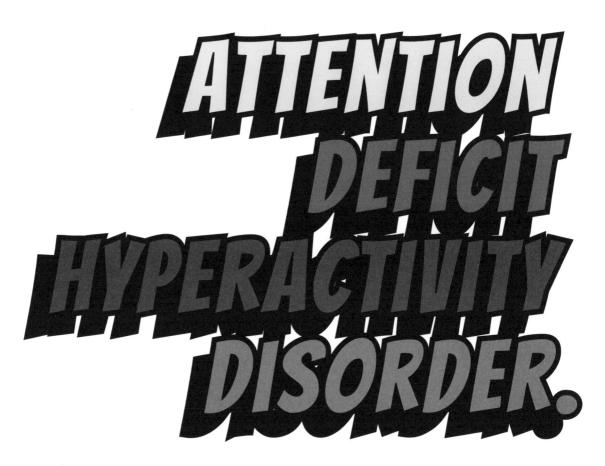

ATTENTION DEFICIT HYPERACTIVITY DISORDER.

See? Really long!

When people have ADHD,
some things are harder
for them to do. That's what
the word "disorder" means.

But it's important to know that there is nothing wrong with people who have ADHD—their brains just process information in a unique way.*

*Like how they think, feel, and experience emotions.

I see ADHD as a

Wanna know why?

Because I have this superpower too!

But more on that later.

ADHD affects **millions of kids** worldwide, and even more grownups.[1]

[1]Jennifer Wirth, "ADHD Statistics and Facts in 2023," ed. Meaghan Harmon, Forbes, August 24, 2023, http://www.forbes.com/health/mind/adhd-statistics

There are lots of ways to help make things easier for people with ADHD. Changes can be made at home or at school, and doctors might suggest therapy or medication to see if it helps.

Exercise, sleep, and eating healthy foods also help me a lot!

ADHD can look like a lot
of different things.

Sometimes people with ADHD
have trouble sitting still or
can appear overexcited.

I've heard this described
as "bouncing off the walls!"

And while that sounds fun...it can be challenging for the person experiencing it, because, often, they *do* want to sit and listen.

People with ADHD can also be described as having their "head in the clouds," which sounds lovely to me!

But what this really means is that it can be

HARD TO CONCENTRATE.

Often, our minds drift off,
so we lose focus.

People with ADHD can also seem forgetful or misplace things.

A task that may appear straightforward to someone else may be difficult for someone with ADHD.

And it can be really hard to

MANAGE
OUR
EMOTIONS.

Sometimes, as a person with ADHD, life can sometimes feel like a long list of

When I was growing up, I didn't understand why I experienced things differently from those around me.

I felt worried, a lot...

I didn't think I was very smart because I would sometimes forget words, or lose my train of thought.

At school, I was often told to stop talking in class, but it wasn't always easy to concentrate on what the teacher was saying— even though I really tried.

Sometimes, I would do or
say things without thinking.

It seemed like words fell out of my mouth before I had even finished thinking them!

And if I thought I had upset someone, I would worry about that, over and over again, for a long time.

OFTEN, MY MIND WAS NOT A HAPPY PLACE TO BE.

It wasn't until I was a grownup that I learned more about ADHD.

A kind doctor explained it to me.

She said what
I was experiencing
was perfectly natural.

RELIEF!

She also made sure I knew
there wasn't anything
wrong with me.

MY BRAIN DIFFERENTLY

JUST WORKS FROM OTHER PEOPLE'S.

And there are lots of others just like me!

I finally understood myself!

I was so relieved, I cried happy tears.

After that, my worry and frustration started to fade.

Although, they pop up every now and then (they're sneaky like that).

But now that I know myself better,
I acknowledge those feelings and
remind myself where they come from.

THIS HELPS ME ACCEPT AND LOVE MYSELF AS I AM.

And now, most of the time,
my mind is a happy place to be!

Oh, and remember how I mentioned ADHD can actually be a superpower?

That's because ADHD doesn't just mean having challenges—it means having a unique way of seeing the world and existing in it.

Like...

When something is super interesting, we can get **fixated*** and lose track of time!

Has that ever happened to you? Maybe with a favorite book, or game, or writing a story?

*Being strongly focused on something for a long period.

This is called "**hyperfocus**," and not only does it signal to us the things we

FEEL MOST PASSIONATE ABOUT,

it can be useful in getting tasks done, too!

ADHD CAN SPARK CREATIVITY.

Our brains need new experiences and ideas to grow—just like our bodies need food and water!

This means when we are creative—drawing, inventing, or dreaming up new ideas—we thrive.

It can be our happy place.

The last thing I want to say is
something I hope you already know.

EVER

DIFFE

YONE
S
RENT.

It's true!

Your strengths, abilities, and how your brain processes information are all unique to you.

Accepting others for who they are is really important—and so is accepting ourselves.

If you have ADHD, it can feel difficult.

But if you do, remember the strengths of your brain, too, because it's amazing and...

UNIQUE

-JUST LIKE YOU!

For caregivers of kids with ADHD:

understood.org

maggiedent.com

aacap.org

witherslackgroup.co.uk

For grownups with ADHD:

chadd.org

add.org

additudemag.com

Outro
for grownups

I hope you loved reading this book, and that it opened up some new areas of understanding for you and the kid you're reading with.

Now, you might be wondering how to continue the conversation with the kid in your life. Here are some questions to reflect on together. I hope they might help your kiddo see and understand themselves or others in a new way.

- What does ADHD mean to you?

- Do you ever feel like you have your head in the clouds, or are bouncing off the walls? Or has a friend told you they feel this way?

- Do you ever feel worried or challenged?

- Are there times when you feel like you need extra support to do tasks or understand new concepts?

- Do you think other people feel this way too?

- What's a kind way we can help other people feel supported and understood?

- What is your superpower?!